Happy Habits Journal

12 Months

12 Habits

One happier you

An undated, guided journal to help you develop 12 positive habits that will make you happier and more resilient.

Karen Brown

DEDICATION

To the two people who have supported me
unconditionally on my journey:

my husband Tony and

my son Daniel.

And to my Dad.

Thank you for fighting for me.

ISBN: 9781730949937

This planner belongs to:

About the Happy Habits Journal

This happiness journal has evolved out of my previous book The Positivity Planner, and whilst there are some minor changes, it's much the same book. The main difference arose from my wish to create something that you could start anytime, not just on January 1st. The other key difference is it doesn't have a space for appointments and such, so it's purely a journal and not a planner.

To support you in your journey I've created a closed Facebook group that you are more than welcome to join:

www.facebook.com/groups/MyPositiveLife

In this free group you'll find:

• Daily dose of positivity quotes

• Weekly post to see if anyone would like some energy healing

• Weekly post to see if anyone would like an oracle card reading

• A weekly check in on the group to see if you need help, have any questions etc

• A monthly live Q&A.

So, pop along and join this supportive community.

Happy Habits

In the field of psychology, much work has been carried out to understand the brain: how it works and why we behave the way we do. The focus has been about helping people with mental health challenges, so that treatments and medicines could be developed to alleviate symptoms, and subsequently help people move back into the community with support.

However, over time, some researchers started to look at what made people happier. Why were some people happier than others? This opened up a whole new field called Positive Psychology. It is from these learnings, and my own experience, that this journal was born. In it, you'll learn to build up 12 habits that have been found to help you feel happier.

Just remember, it takes time to build a habit, so start small, and gradually build you habit muscles. Don't beat yourself if they don't stick. It can take anywhere from 14 days to several months for a habit to form.

The other thing to remember is to focus on building one habit, and only that habit, for the month.

If you miss one or two days or weeks, that's ok. Pick it up again. If you feel some resistance to the habit, consider sharing this in the group. You'll find that you're not alone, and perhaps we can help and support you to move past it.

This is a summary of the habits for the year, and the reasoning behind them:

Month 1 – Decluttering

Having too much stuff is stressful and a massive cause of anxiety for some people. So, in this month we let go of what we don't need or like, to make space for something new. The less you have, the less you'll have to look after and the more time you'll have for yourself. You're not only reducing what you own, you'll save money and time.

Month 2 – Gratitude

When you focus on your blessings, you realise how truly blessed you are. Research shows that those who keep a gratitude journal have improved levels of happiness. Even those who started keeping the journal, and stopped after 21 days, still had higher levels of happiness months later.

Month 3 – Meditation

Meditation has been around for centuries. It's a wonderful practice that helps to quieten the mind, helps you relax and take time out for yourself. Even practicing for 5 or 10 minutes a day is beneficial.

Month 4 – Forgiveness

Not just others but also yourself. Release yourself from a painful time, event or person. Forgiveness doesn't necessarily mean you absolve the person, just that you're severing the ties to the pain. It's also a time to ask for forgiveness and say you're sorry.

Month 5 – Kindness

Not just to others but also to yourself. Being kind has been shown to have loads of health benefits, the most notable is the release of serotonin. Serotonin has been linked to feelings of well-being and happiness.

Month 6 – Self-care

Because you cannot serve from an empty cup. Self-care can take many forms, from making time for exercise, watching your diet, or visiting the dentist to booking in for a retreat or spa weekend. It's about making you a priority in your own life.

Month 7 – Journaling

Make a date with yourself, and then take time to work through your day. Write it down, let it out and then let it go. It's also a great practice for thinking things through, focusing your thoughts and developing a positive mindset.

Month 8 – Visualisation.

It may sound crazy, but your brain doesn't distinguish between what's happened, and what you think has happened. By visualising your day or your success, you're one step closer to making it happen.

Month 9 – Optimism

Because optimists are happier and healthier. If you don't like positive affirmations, try optimistic affirmations instead.

Month 10 – Learning

Whether it's reading, listening to an audiobook or podcast, or watching a documentary on tv or YouTube, learn something new this month and feed your mind. You could even just challenge yourself to watch a TED talk a day for however ling this month is.

Month 11 – Creating

Take time to do or try something creative. Whether it's a colouring book, learning to knit or writing a blog, get creative and make something. Try and come up with something different, or maybe try something you've wanted to do for a long time but haven't gotten around to.

Month 12 – Fun.

Take time to rediscover what fun is to you. Whether it simply splashing in puddles, going to a show, singing, dancing or meeting up with friends, make this last month count, and have fun doing it.

Before you start

Take a minute to think about how happy you are right now. On a scale of 1 to 10, where 1 is totally miserable and 10 is blissfully happy, how would you score?

Today my happiness score is: ____

A quick note

Because this journal is undated, I have included 5 whole weeks for each month. So, start on the day of the week that is relevant for that month, and carry on until the end month. You could even cross out the days that aren't relevant for that month. So, if the month starts on a Wednesday, cross out Monday and Tuesday at the start of the month and start from Wednesday.

Additionally, because the journal is undated, don't feel that you have to follow the order of the book. This is the order that I found most beneficial for me, but if you'd prefer to start with gratitude because it's something that you've done before, then by all means change the order that you do each month in. Just enjoy the journey.

Also, there are some suggested tools, books and links. These are just suggestions and the author has no affiliation with any of the people or pages recommended.

About Karen Brown

Karen Brown is a life coach, meditation teacher, energy healer, trainer and author.

She believes that there are certain things that are essential for a purposeful and happy life, and it's her job to help you find your version of what that is. She loves helping people, and does this through her books, training courses and by her coaching packages.

For each of the happy habits she is developing 90-day journals for those who want to maintain a specific habit, and e-courses for those who want to dig deeper into a specific habit.

If you might benefit from some energy healing and/or life coaching with Karen, then visit her website and book a free 1:1 chat

She also publishes a daily dose of positivity on her social media accounts and via email.

You can connect with her via:

- Her website: coachkarenbrown.com
- Her Facebook page: @coachkarenbrown
- Her Twitter account: @coachkarenbrown
- She is also on LinkedIn, Pinterest and Instagram.

Each year, she sets herself 100 goals, and you can learn more about these on her blog. In 2019, she actual set herself 119 goals.

Month 1 - Decluttering

Happiness is not having what you want.

It is appreciating what you have.

Anon

In Month 1, our focus is on decluttering. Why? Well, by decluttering your home, you're creating space for whatever you'd like to come to you in the new year. The other benefit of decluttering is by reducing the amount of stuff you have, you have less to tidy up, freeing your time. Once you get into the habit of buying only the things that bring you joy, you'll begin to live in a home full of all the stuff that you really love.

What is clutter?

Clutter is simply having too much stuff for the space that you have. If you're a Hollywood movie star, and own a big mansion, then you may well have room to store hundreds of clothes, shoes and handbags, but realistically speaking, most of us have very limited space, so we need to prioritise what we keep.

Decluttering is simply the conscious decision to keep the stuff that we really need on a day to day basis and the stuff that we love. Once you've removed the excess then you have a home full of the things that mean the most to you and the things you value most.

How to declutter

There are several different methods for decluttering your home. So, choose the one that feels right to you.

I've found that combining Marie Kondo's method of decluttering by type of stuff, with a room by room approach, you remove the possibility of just moving things around your house.

Start by tidying up your home and putting everything back in its rightful place. Then start upstairs, moving downstairs then the garage, garden and sheds/summerhouse. Personally, I'd start with the bathrooms for a quick win, and then move to the bedroom, but you can start with your bedroom, decluttering your wardrobe, accessories, make up, jewellery etc and then whatever is left in the room.

On my website, under the resources tab, you'll find my free downloadable e-book and some worksheets that will help you assess how cluttered/uncluttered you are and make a plan to tackle it.

Releasing your unwanted clutter

When you let things go, they have to go somewhere! Realistically, you can only do one of three things:

- Bin it
- Give it away
- Sell it

Only bin things that no-one else will have a use for. If you're going to give stuff away, then think of your friends, family and favourite charity shops. Where things may have some sort of value, then consider selling them through:

- eBay
- Facebook marketplace
- Auction houses.

You may have to pay fees, but you can use the money to buy something that will bring you joy in your clean, tidy and decluttered home.

My goal for this month is to declutter...

_____

_____

_____

_____

_____

_____

To do this, I will...

_____

_____

_____

_____

_____

_____

Planning for success

What are the benefits of trying this habit?

_____

_____

What things might stop you this month?

_____

_____

What could you do about them to stop them being a problem?

_____

_____

How will you know you've been successful this month?

_____

_____

How will you reward yourself for that success?

_____

_____

"The secret of getting ahead is getting started."
Mark Twain

Week commencing: _____

Monday
Today, I released

Tuesday
Today, I let go of

Wednesday
Today, I decluttered

Thursday

Today, I released

Friday

Today, I let go of

Saturday

Today, I decluttered

Sunday

Today, I set free

"For me it is sufficient to have a corner by my hearth, a book and a friend…"

Fernandez de Andrada

Week commencing: _____

Monday

Today, I released

Tuesday

Today, I let go of

Wednesday

Today, I decluttered

Thursday

Today, I released

Friday

Today, I let go of

Saturday

Today, I decluttered

Sunday

Today, I set free

"He who knows that enough is enough will always have enough."

Lao Tzu

Week commencing: _____

Monday

Today, I released

Tuesday

Today, I let go of

Wednesday

Today, I decluttered

Thursday

Today, I released

Friday

Today, I let go of

Saturday

Today, I decluttered

Sunday

Today, I set free

"Your worth consists in what you are and not in what you have.

Thomas A. Edison

Week commencing: _____

Monday

> Today, I released

Tuesday

> Today, I let go of

Wednesday

> Today, I decluttered

Thursday

Today, I released

Friday

Today, I let go of

Saturday

Today, I decluttered

Sunday

Today, I set free

"Do not overrate what you have received, nor envy others. He who envies others does not obtain peace of mind."

Buddha

Week commencing: _____

Monday

> Today, I released

Tuesday

> Today, I let go of

Wednesday

> Today, I decluttered

Thursday

Today, I released

Friday

Today, I let go of

Saturday

Today, I decluttered

Sunday

Today, I set free

Reflections on your month of decluttering

What went well for you this month and why was this?

_____

_____

_____

What didn't go well for you and why?

_____

_____

_____

What would you have done differently?

_____

_____

_____

How will you adopt this habit in the future?

_____

_____

_____

Now again, on a scale of 1 to 10, where 1 is totally miserable and 10 is blissfully happy, what would you rate your level of happiness right now?

Today my happiness score is: ____

Is there any difference between when you started the month and when you finished the month?

Did decluttering your home increase your sense of happiness?

_____

_____

_____

Why do you think that was?

_____

_____

_____

If you haven't finished decluttering, then keep going and ask for support in the group.

There is a 90-day Decluttering Journal that may help support you on Karen Brown's Amazon page:

www.amazon.co.uk/Karen-Brown/e/B00AXAF2M8

Month 2 - Gratitude

The essence of all beautiful art, all great art, is gratitude.

Friedrich Nietzsche

Month 2 is our month of gratitude. You may also think of it as your month of thankfulness or one for counting your blessings.

So, why have I chosen gratitude and included it so early as a habit?

Quite simply because practicing gratitude makes you happier.

It's true. This simple practice is one that has long lasting effects and is so easy to adopt.

These days we're so busy running around, we don't take time to stop and take stock of where we are and how we got there. By taking 5 minutes each day to take note of the good things in your life, the positive people, experiences and events present every day, you help build your positivity muscle. The more you do this, the more you notice things that you might have previously taken for granted.

The more you notice how much that you have to be grateful for, the happier you feel.

Research by Robert Emmons found that practicing gratitude for just 21 days had long lasting effects, even when the person no longer practiced it.

He also found that the positive effects of gratitude impacted not just the persons mental and spiritual health, but also, their physical health. The reason for this seems to be that by being grateful for what you have and realising how much you have to be grateful for lowers your stress levels, which has a knock-on effect on your physical health.

Gratitude has two components:

1. The affirmation that good things have occurred and that there is goodness in this world. This is so important when there is so much negativity in the press and online.
2. The recognition of where those good things came from. Whether it was a gift to yourself, from a friend or from a stranger, or even from a higher power, whatever you are thankful for, you were deserving of that gift.

Emmons suggested several ways to embrace gratitude. Not just by keeping a gratitude diary, although that is a big part of it, but also by saying thank you to people.

You can find out more about Robert Emmons and his research into the impact of gratitude by visiting his profile page at Berkley:

greatergood.berkeley.edu/profile/robert_emmons

This page includes links to a number of his posts on the subject of gratitude and thankfulness. He has also written a number of books.

How do I start?

1. Start by committing to how many things you will be grateful for each day. At the beginning, start with being grateful for just 3 things. (This is what I have included in this planner). As you start to realise how much you actually have to be grateful for, you may want to increase this to 5 things and then maybe 10 things. (This is how many things Oprah Winfrey says she does.)
2. Choose what you're going to use, whether it's a planner like this, a notepad or a really pretty notebook, have a special place to write down your thoughts. I've published a simple 90-Day Gratitude Journal on Amazon if you'd like to continue with this habit.
3. Choose what time of the day you will complete your journal. First thing in the morning, or last thing at night are usually the best times.
4. Commit to giving thanks for different things each day. To start with, you'll probably be grateful for the people in your life, the place you live and the skills you have. As you continue, you'll notice smaller things, and as you continue, you'll notice even more.
5. If you want to, choose colourful gel pens, or what I do, use glitter pens.
6. Just write.

Before you start, on a scale of 1 to 10, where 10 is totally happy, and 1 is deeply depressed, what would you rate your level of happiness right now?

Today, I rate my happiness as:

Planning for success

What are the benefits of trying this habit?

_____

_____

What things might stop you this month?

_____

_____

What could you do about them to stop them being a problem?

_____

_____

How will you know you've been successful this month?

_____

_____

How will you reward yourself for that success?

_____

_____

"Reflect upon your present blessings, of which man has many."

Charles Dickens

Week commencing: _____

Monday
Today, I am grateful for:

_____

_____

_____

Tuesday
Today, I am thankful for:

_____

_____

_____

Wednesday
Today, I am deeply grateful for:

_____

_____

_____

Thursday
Today, I am grateful for:

_____

_____

_____

Friday
Today, I am thankful for:

_____

_____

_____

Saturday
Today, I give thanks for:

_____

_____

_____

Sunday
Today, I am deeply grateful for:

_____

_____

_____

"The happiness of life is made up of the little charities of a kiss or smile, a kind look, a heartfelt compliment."

Samuel Taylor Coleridge

Week commencing: _____

Monday
Today, I am grateful for:

_____

_____

_____

Tuesday
Today, I am thankful for:

_____

_____

_____

Wednesday
Today, I am deeply grateful for:

_____

_____

_____

Thursday
Today, I am grateful for:

_____

_____

_____

Friday
Today, I am thankful for:

_____

_____

_____

Saturday
Today, I give thanks for:

_____

_____

_____

Sunday
Today, I am deeply grateful for:

_____

_____

_____

"The secret of happiness is to count your blessings..."
William Penn

Week commencing: _____

Monday
Today, I am grateful for:

_____

_____

_____

Tuesday
Today, I am thankful for:

_____

_____

_____

Wednesday
Today, I am deeply grateful for:

_____

_____

_____

Thursday
Today, I am grateful for:

_____

_____

_____

Friday
Today, I am thankful for:

_____

_____

_____

Saturday
Today, I give thanks for:

_____

_____

_____

Sunday
Today, I am deeply grateful for:

_____

_____

_____

"Gratitude is not only the greatest of virtues, but the parent of all others."

Marcus Tullius Cicero

Week commencing: _____

Monday
Today, I am grateful for:

_____

_____

_____

Tuesday
Today, I am thankful for:

_____

_____

_____

Wednesday
Today, I am deeply grateful for:

_____

_____

_____

Thursday
Today, I am grateful for:

_____

_____

_____

Friday
Today, I am thankful for:

_____

_____

_____

Saturday
Today, I give thanks for:

_____

_____

_____

Sunday
Today, I am deeply grateful for:

_____

_____

_____

"It is not the length of life, but the depth of life."
Ralph Waldo Emmerson

Week commencing: _____

Monday
Today, I am grateful for:

_____

_____

_____

Tuesday
Today, I am thankful for:

_____

_____

_____

Wednesday
Today, I am deeply grateful for:

_____

_____

_____

Thursday
Today, I am grateful for:

_____

_____

_____

Friday
Today, I am thankful for:

_____

_____

_____

Saturday
Today, I give thanks for:

_____

_____

_____

Sunday
Today, I am deeply grateful for:

_____

_____

_____

Reflections on your month of gratitude

What went well for you this month and why was this?

_____

_____

_____

What didn't go well for you and why?

_____

_____

_____

What would you have done differently?

_____

_____

_____

How will you adopt this habit in the future?

_____

_____

_____

Now again, on a scale of 1 to 10, where 1 is totally miserable and 10 is blissfully happy, what would you rate your level of happiness right now?

Today my happiness score is: ____

Is there any difference between when you started the month and when you finished the month?

Did practicing gratitude increase your sense of happiness?

_____

_____

_____

Why do you think that was?

_____

_____

_____

If you would like to maintain the gratitude habit then you just need a notebook, however, there is a 90-day Gratitude Journal that you may like on Karen Brown's Amazon page:

www.amazon.co.uk/Karen-Brown/e/B00AXAF2M8

Month 3 - Meditation

Half an hour's meditation each day is essential, except when you are busy.

Then a full hour is needed.

Saint Francis de Sales

Month 3 is our month to develop the meditation habit.

Meditation is very much like prayer, however, when you pray you talk to God, when you meditate, you try and listen instead.

So, what is meditation?

Meditation is a powerful de-stressor where you use one or more techniques such as chanting, focusing on an object/action or someone else's voice, to find a state of deep peace, clarity and relaxation.

Meditation is one of my cornerstone positive practices that I hope will become part of your day too.

I find that by taking 10 minutes in the morning to quieten my mind, I am much more focused during the day and creative ideas to flow much more easily.

If I can't sleep, I'll stick on a guided meditation and find that my mind starts to quieten down, and sleep comes.

Whether you choose to start or end the day with a quiet meditation is up to you. However, spending just 5 minutes a day, focusing on your breath, letting your mind empty and allowing yourself time to relax completely has many long-term benefits.

Think of all the illnesses stress creates such as high blood pressure, heart disease, loss of sleep, anxiety and so on. A de-stressor like meditation has the opposite effect, and you don't need to take medication to benefit from it.

There have been numerous studies to back this up. If you'd like to learn more, go to:

www.healthline.com/nutrition/12-benefits-of-meditation

Creating a space to meditate

To start meditating you need:

A quiet space

Somewhere where you'll be comfortable for example you may want to lie down on your bed or a yoga mat, or you may prefer a recliner chair.

Alternatively, you could buy a zafu, which is a type of cushion.

Consider having a blanket to keep you warm.

I also use a bolster cushion to support the backs of my legs.

Some relaxing music. You may find music or even guided meditations via YouTube.

If you think that you may fall asleep, and you need to stay awake, consider setting an alarm to let you know when it's time to stop.

How do you meditate?

There are several meditation techniques available to you, including guided meditations, chanting and by focusing on a something, like a flame.

The aim is to focus your thoughts on one thing, like your breathing or a chant. When you do this, other thoughts start to float away. However, like anything it takes practice, so don't be surprised if other thoughts come into your mind, acknowledge them, but then focus back on your breathing.

To start with, try some of the guided meditations you can download or find on YouTube. They have different thing they focus on, so choose one that appeals to you.

One of my favourite ways to meditate is to listen to music with a simple chant and then repeat that chant in my head.

During the month, I suggest that you try different methods and then find the ones that appeal to you most or suit your lifestyle.

Getting started

I'll be posting different meditations for you to try out in our Facebook group:

www.facebook.com/groups/MyPositiveYear

Check out the "Units" section, as well as posts.

You may find that there are meditation classes being run near you.

Planning for success

What are the benefits of trying this habit?

_____

_____

What things might stop you this month?

_____

_____

What could you do about them to stop them being a problem?

_____

_____

How will you know you've been successful this month?

_____

_____

How will you reward yourself for that success?

_____

_____

"Nothing that is worth knowing can be taught."
Oscar Wilde

Week commencing: _____

Monday

Today, I meditated for _____ mins
Using

Tuesday

Today, I meditated for _____ mins
Using

Wednesday

Today, I meditated for _____ mins
using

Thursday

Today, I meditated for _____ mins using

Friday

Today, I meditated for _____ mins using

Saturday

Today, I meditated for _____ mins using

Sunday

Today, I meditated for _____ mins using

"Knowing is not enough; we must apply. Willing is not enough, we must do."
                                        Johann Wolfgang von Goethe

Week commencing: _____

Monday
Today, I meditated for _____ mins Using

Tuesday
Today, I meditated for _____ mins Using

Wednesday
Today, I meditated for _____ mins using

Thursday

Today, I meditated for _____ mins
using

Friday

Today, I meditated for _____ mins
using

Saturday

Today, I meditated for _____ mins
using

Sunday

Today, I meditated for _____ mins
using

"It takes two to speak truth, one to speak and another to hear."

Henry David Thoreau

Week commencing: _____

Monday

Today, I meditated for _____ mins
Using

Tuesday

Today, I meditated for _____ mins
Using

Wednesday

Today, I meditated for _____ mins
using

Thursday

Today, I meditated for _____ mins
using

Friday

Today, I meditated for _____ mins
using

Saturday

Today, I meditated for _____ mins
using

Sunday

Today, I meditated for _____ mins
using

"Truth, and goodness, and beauty are but different faces of the same All."

Ralph Waldo Emmerson

Week commencing: _____

Monday

Today, I meditated for _____ mins
Using

Tuesday

Today, I meditated for _____ mins
Using

Wednesday

Today, I meditated for _____ mins
using

Thursday

Today, I meditated for _____ mins
using

Friday

Today, I meditated for _____ mins
using

Saturday

Today, I meditated for _____ mins
using

Sunday

Today, I meditated for _____ mins
using

"If you want to be happy, be."

Leo Tolstoy

Week commencing: _____

Monday

Today, I meditated for _____ mins
Using

Tuesday

Today, I meditated for _____ mins
Using

Wednesday

Today, I meditated for _____ mins
using

Thursday

Today, I meditated for _____ mins using

Friday

Today, I meditated for _____ mins using

Saturday

Today, I meditated for _____ mins using

Sunday

Today, I meditated for _____ mins using

Reflections on your month of meditation

What went well for you this month and why was this?

_____

_____

_____

What didn't go well for you and why?

_____

_____

_____

What would you have done differently?

_____

_____

_____

How will you adopt this habit in the future?

_____

_____

_____

Now again, on a scale of 1 to 10, where 1 is totally miserable and 10 is blissfully happy, what would you rate your level of happiness right now?

Today my happiness score is: ____

Is there any difference between when you started the month and when you finished the month?

Did practicing meditation increase your sense of happiness?

_____

_____

_____

Why do you think that was?

_____

_____

_____

If you would like to maintain the gratitude habit then you just need a notebook, however, there is a 90-day Gratitude Journal that you may like on Karen Brown's Amazon page:

www.amazon.co.uk/Karen-Brown/e/B00AXAF2M8

Month 4 - Forgiveness

The err is human, to forgive divine

Alexander Pope

Month 4 is our month to develop the forgiveness habit.

So why have I chosen forgiveness as a positive habit?

Well, if you can let go of some of the negative energy around the hurts of the past, you will lighten your load, begin the process of healing your spirit and be able to move forward much more easily.

Saying this, forgiveness is a trait of the strong. It takes strength to say: "I forgive you", and it takes even more strength to say sorry, and ask for forgiveness.

There is a wonderful course by Nobel Peace Prize winner Archbishop Desmond Tutu, which explains what forgiveness is and isn't and introduces a simple 4 step process to forgive someone. You can sign up for this 30-day course at:

www.forgivenesschallenge.com

What is forgiveness?

Forgiveness is the conscious act of pardoning someone so that you no longer feel pain and anger or attach blame to something that happened.

The person may not be worthy of forgiveness, but this is a process of releasing you from the pain of what happened.

It doesn't absolve them.

What forgiveness isn't?

Forgiveness isn't about forgetting what a person did, or not asking for justice for yourself. It is about releasing yourself from the connections that bind you, so that you can begin the process of healing.

How can you forgive someone?

This is the simple 4 step process in the forgiveness course, that was originally set out by Desmond and Mpho Tutu in their book "The Book of Forgiving. The fourfold path for healing ourselves and our world" and used in the Truth and Reconciliation Tribunals in South Africa.

1. Tell your story
2. Name your hurt
3. Forgive
4. Renew or release the relationship

You can do this by talking to the person concerned if this is possible, by journaling or by visualising it, and sending the energy out into the universe.

This isn't an easy habit to get into, so start small and very gradually build up your forgiveness muscle.

As you build up your practice, you may want to look at forgiving bigger and bigger hurts from your past.

Do this at a pace that suits you.

It may be that as you forgive people, something comes up that knocks you off balance, so if you feel the need to take a step back, then do so.

The more you can forgive, the lighter your load, and the more you can move forward.

An alternative method of forgiving someone

As a healer, when I send out distance healing, I set my intentions and send them out to the universe. You can do this with forgiveness.

In this activity, you're sending out your intention to forgive someone and also ask them for forgiveness. So, try this:

> It is my intention to send love, light and healing energy to xxx and to forgive them for anything they did to hurt me, whether it was their intention or not. I release myself from this pain.

> It is my intention to ask for forgiveness for anything that I did to hurt xxx, whether it was intended or not. I ask that the universe sends this request from my heart to theirs, so that they know that I ask their forgiveness.

Sending out this energy is especially useful if the person you want to forgive or ask forgiveness from has passed away.

Planning for success

What are the benefits of trying this habit?

_____

_____

What things might stop you this month?

_____

_____

What could you do about them to stop them being a problem?

_____

_____

How will you know you've been successful this month?

_____

_____

How will you reward yourself for that success?

_____

_____

"I have learned more from my mistakes than from my success."

Sir Humphry Davy

Week commencing: _____

Monday

Today, I forgive
For:

Tuesday

Today, I forgive
For:

Wednesday

Today, I forgive
For:

Thursday

Today, I forgive
For:

Friday

Today, I forgive
For:

Saturday

Today, I forgive
For:

Sunday

Today, I forgive
For:

"The weak can never forgive. Forgiveness is the attribute of the strong."

— Mahatma Gandhi

Week commencing: _____

Monday

Today, I forgive
For:

Tuesday

Today, I forgive
For:

Wednesday

Today, I forgive
For:

Thursday

Today, I forgive
For:

Friday

Today, I forgive
For:

Saturday

Today, I forgive
For:

Sunday

Today, I forgive
For:

"For every minute you are angry you lose sixty seconds of happiness."

Ralph Waldo Emmerson

Week commencing: _____

Monday

Today, I forgive
For:

Tuesday

Today, I forgive
For:

Wednesday

Today, I forgive
For:

Thursday

Today, I forgive
For:

Friday

Today, I forgive
For:

Saturday

Today, I forgive
For:

Sunday

Today, I forgive
For:

"Forgiveness is the fragrance that the violet sheds on the heel that has crushed it."

Mark Twain

Week commencing: _____

Monday

Today, I forgive
For:

Tuesday

Today, I forgive
For:

Wednesday

Today, I forgive
For:

Thursday

Today, I forgive
For:

Friday

Today, I forgive
For:

Saturday

Today, I forgive
For:

Sunday

Today, I forgive
For:

"Every day, in every way, I am getting better and better."

Émile Coué

Week commencing: _____

Monday

Today, I forgive
For:

Tuesday

Today, I forgive
For:

Wednesday

Today, I forgive
For:

Thursday

Today, I forgive
For:

Friday

Today, I forgive
For:

Saturday

Today, I forgive
For:

Sunday

Today, I forgive
For:

Reflections on your month of forgiveness

What went well for you this month and why was this?

_____

_____

_____

What didn't go well for you and why?

_____

_____

_____

What would you have done differently?

_____

_____

_____

How will you adopt this habit in the future?

_____

_____

_____

Now again, on a scale of 1 to 10, where 1 is totally miserable and 10 is blissfully happy, what would you rate your level of happiness right now?

Today my happiness score is: ____

Is there any difference between when you started the month and when you finished the month?

Did practicing forgiveness increase your sense of happiness?

_____

_____

_____

Why do you think that was?

_____

_____

_____

Month 5 - Kindness

Kindness in words creates confidence.
Kindness in thinking creates profoundness.
Kindness in giving creates love.

Lao Tzu

Month 5 is our month to develop the kindness habit. Not just being kind to others, but also being kind to ourselves.

What is kindness?

When you look at definitions of what kindness is, you'll find words such as:

- friendly
- generous
- considerate
- respectful
- helpful
- gentle
- caring.

Never underestimate the impact you have on other people, so let's take this month and make it a positive impact, every single day.

The benefits of being kind to others

As well as giving you a warm feeling inside, Dr David R Hamilton (author of "The Five Side Effects of Kindness") found significant benefits to both your physical and mental health as a result of being kind to someone else. Happy hormones like serotonin, oxytocin and endorphins got released. Blood pressure goes down and you just feel happier.

In addition, a study by the University of British Columbia found that after a group of people were kind 6 days a week for a month, they were happier, more positive and had better relationships than before, possibly because people like people who are kind to them.

Being kind to others

Your act of kindness may be big or small, unplanned and random, or part of a conscious effort that you repeat for example donating to a specific charity. It really doesn't matter. It is the act itself, repeated daily, that has the impact.

Some examples I found at:

www.randomactsofkindness.org

include:

- get dinner ready for someone who usually cooks
- wash the dishes without being asked
- send a thank you card
- show someone that you appreciate them
- tell someone how they've inspired you. They probably didn't know.
- help someone in need
- give someone a compliment
- donate food to a foodbank or animal charity
- check in on someone. Visit them or give them a ring.
- take someone out for coffee
- visit someone lonely in hospital or a nursing home
- sign up to volunteer in an area you're good at
- post a positive comment on social media
- say thank you to someone who has served you. This could be anyone from the person who delivers your mail or your meal, to a member of the armed services.

Now think about the number of ways that you could be kind this month.

How could I be kind this month?

_____

_____

_____

_____

_____

Being kind to yourself

As part of this month of kindness, I really think it would be nice if you could take at least one week out of the month to be kind to yourself as well. This includes how you talk to yourself and about yourself.

How could you be kind to yourself?

Take a few minutes to think about how you could be kind to yourself. What would that feel like?

_____

_____

_____

_____

_____

Planning for success

What are the benefits of trying this habit?

_____

_____

What things might stop you this month?

_____

_____

What could you do about them to stop them being a problem?

_____

_____

How will you know you've been successful this month?

_____

_____

How will you reward yourself for that success?

_____

_____

"No act of kindness, however small, is ever wasted."
Aesop

Week commencing: _____

Monday

Today, I was kind by

Tuesday

Today, I was kind to

Wednesday

Today, I was kind to

Thursday

Today I was kind because

Friday

Today I was kind to

Saturday

Today I was kind by

Sunday

Today I was kind to

"Be kind, for everyone you meet is fighting a harder battle."

Plato

Week commencing: _____

Monday

Today, I was kind by

Tuesday

Today, I was kind to

Wednesday

Today, I was kind to

Thursday

Today I was kind because

Friday

Today I was kind to

Saturday

Today I was kind by

Sunday

Today I was kind to

"Kindness is a language which the deaf can hear and the blind can see."

Mark Twain

Week commencing: _____

Monday

Today, I was kind by

Tuesday

Today, I was kind to

Wednesday

Today, I was kind to

Thursday

Today I was kind because

Friday

Today I was kind to

Saturday

Today I was kind by

Sunday

Today I was kind to

"So many gods, so many creeds, so many paths that wind and wind, while just the art of being kind, Is all the sad world needs."

Ella Wheeler Wilcox

Week commencing: _____

Monday

Today, I was kind by

Tuesday

Today, I was kind to

Wednesday

Today, I was kind to

Thursday

Today I was kind because

Friday

Today I was kind to

Saturday

Today I was kind by

Sunday

Today I was kind to

"Everything has beauty, but not everyone sees it."
Confucius

Week commencing: _____

Monday

Today, I was kind by

Tuesday

Today, I was kind to

Wednesday

Today, I was kind to

Thursday

Today I was kind because

Friday

Today I was kind to

Saturday

Today I was kind by

Sunday

Today I was kind to

Reflections on your month of kindness

What went well for you this month and why was this?

_____

_____

_____

What didn't go well for you and why?

_____

_____

_____

What would you have done differently?

_____

_____

_____

How will you adopt this habit in the future?

_____

_____

_____

Now again, on a scale of 1 to 10, where 1 is totally miserable and 10 is blissfully happy, what would you rate your level of happiness right now?

Today my happiness score is: ____

Is there any difference between when you started the month and when you finished the month?

Did practicing kindness increase your sense of happiness?

_____

_____

_____

Why do you think that was?

_____

_____

_____

Month 6 – Self Care

To keep the body in good health is a duty...
otherwise we shall not be able to keep our
mind strong and clear.

Buddha

Month 6 is our month to focus on self-care.

It's the month where you get to put your needs first and recharge your batteries.

The old adage "you can't serve from an empty cup" is so true. It's also why you're told to put your own oxygen mask on before you help others. You can only serve if you're around to do so, and yet so many of us neglect our own needs in favour of others.

Get into the habit this month of making time for yourself and putting your own needs first. Think about what self-care means to you.

It's not about pampering or going to the spa every weekend. It goes much deeper than that. It's about your physical, mental, emotional and spiritual health.

So, before we start the month, let's take a minute to think about your health.

Your Physical Health

This includes taking time to eat properly and get some exercise. However, it also includes catching up on those appointments you've been putting off for example the doctor, dentist or optician.

Your mental health

Your mental health is about how you process what's happening to you and around you.

One thing my own life coach did with me is worked on boundaries. What she had me do is create a rulebook for me. This included things such as how I should be treated by other people, what was acceptable and what wasn't. It was then up to me to enforce those boundaries.

So, perhaps one of the things you could do for yourself this month is create your own "Rulebook of me". If you need to, use a separate sheet of paper.

Your emotional health

Your emotional health includes how you express yourself, for example how you react in stressful situations.

In some of the previous months some of the activities we've covered include ways to reduce your stress and increase your levels of happiness.

Your spiritual health

This is about your relationship with your God, the universe or whoever you worship, and how you express it. This may be in the form of prayer, living by the tenets of your religion or your own moral code.

Whatever you do this month, think about what you can do to look after yourself.

Don't forget, you can reach out for support anytime in the Facebook group.

My Self-care activities this month will include:

_____

_____

_____

_____

_____

My rulebook of me

_____

_____

_____

_____

_____

_____

_____

_____

_____

Planning for success

What are the benefits of trying this habit?

_____

_____

What things might stop you this month?

_____

_____

What could you do about them to stop them being a problem?

_____

_____

How will you know you've been successful this month?

_____

_____

How will you reward yourself for that success?

_____

_____

"Good health and good sense are two of life's greatest blessings."

Publilius Syrus

Week commencing: _____

Monday
Today, I took care of me by

Tuesday
Today, I took care of myself by

Wednesday
Today, I took care of me by

Thursday

Today, I took care of me by

Friday

Today, I took care of myself by

Saturday

Today, I took care of me by

Sunday

Today, I took care of myself by

"An empty lantern provides no light. Self-care is the fuel that allows your light to shine brightly."

Unknown

Week commencing: _____

Monday

Today, I took care of me by

Tuesday

Today, I took care of myself by

Wednesday

Today, I took care of me by

Thursday

Today, I took care of me by

Friday

Today, I took care of myself by

Saturday

Today, I took care of me by

Sunday

Today, I took care of myself by

"The first wealth is health"

Ralph Waldo Emmerson

Week commencing: _____

Monday

Today, I took care of me by

Tuesday

Today, I took care of myself by

Wednesday

Today, I took care of me by

Thursday

Today, I took care of me by

Friday

Today, I took care of myself by

Saturday

Today, I took care of me by

Sunday

Today, I took care of myself by

"It is health that is real wealth and not pieces of gold and silver"

Mahatma Gandhi

Week commencing: _____

Monday

Today, I took care of me by

Tuesday

Today, I took care of myself by

Wednesday

Today, I took care of me by

Thursday

Today, I took care of me by

Friday

Today, I took care of myself by

Saturday

Today, I took care of me by

Sunday

Today, I took care of myself by

"Happiness depends upon us."

Aristotle

Week commencing: _____

Monday

Today, I took care of me by

Tuesday

Today, I took care of myself by

Wednesday

Today, I took care of me by

Thursday

Today, I took care of me by

Friday

Today, I took care of myself by

Saturday

Today, I took care of me by

Sunday

Today, I took care of myself by

Reflections on your month of self-care

What went well for you this month and why was this?

_____

_____

_____

What didn't go well for you and why?

_____

_____

_____

What would you have done differently?

_____

_____

_____

How will you adopt this habit in the future?

_____

_____

_____

Now again, on a scale of 1 to 10, where 1 is totally miserable and 10 is blissfully happy, what would you rate your level of happiness right now?

Today my happiness score is: ____

Is there any difference between when you started the month and when you finished the month?

Did practicing self-care increase your sense of happiness?

_____

_____

_____

Why do you think that was?

_____

_____

_____

Month 7 - Journaling

The art of writing is the art of discovering what you believe.

Gustave Flaubert

Month 7 is our month to develop the journaling habit.

At its simplest, a journal is a record of a day's activities. It can take the form of a bullet list, a brain dump or anything you want it to be. For the purposes of this month, I've given you a page a day, so that you have space to write what you'd like.

Some people use journal prompts to get them writing. These maybe a question, a list or a finish this sentence kind of prompt. Whatever you choose, make it personal, make time each day and try different things until you get into your stride. Hopefully, by the end of the month, you'll not only have the journaling habit, you'll also find the style of journaling that suits you.

Personally, my journal is part ideas book, part brain dump, part lists and parts reflection.

Just remember:

There are no rules.

There is no right way or wrong way.

There is just your way.

Also, don't stress about seeing a blank page. If you can't think about what to write, then just write "I don't know what to write" until the blockage clears.

Don't forget, there is support in the Facebook group.

Journal prompts from the internet...

My favourite tv character is

10 Things I want to do before I die

10 Things I wished I'd said

10 People that inspire me

10 Places that I want to visit

My biggest dream is to

I truly miss....and wish I told them....

My biggest regret is...

Today, I

If my day was a picture, it would look like this...

My favourite quote of the day is...

If I won the lottery, I would...

If money were no object, I would...

If I had the chance, I would tell my 10 year old self...

In 10 years', time, I would like to be able to say I did...

10 ways I love to have fun

10 things I've learnt

My favourite people to visit are

My favourite places to visit are

Planning for success

What are the benefits of trying this habit?

_____

_____

What things might stop you this month?

_____

_____

What could you do about them to stop them being a problem?

_____

_____

How will you know you've been successful this month?

_____

_____

How will you reward yourself for that success?

_____

_____

"What a wee little part of a person's life are his acts and his words! His real life is led in his head and is known to none but himself.

Mark Twain

Date: _____

"Don't judge each day by the harvest you reap but by the seeds that you plant."

Robert Louis Stevenson

Date: _____

"Good humour is one of the best articles of dress one can wear in society."

William Makepeace Thackery

Date: _____

"Begin at the beginning… and go on till you come to the end: then stop."

Lewis Carroll

Date: _____

"You, yourself, as much as anybody in the entire universe, deserve your love and affection."

Buddha

Date: _____

"There are two ways of spreading light: to be the candle or the mirror that reflects it."

Edith Wharton

Date: _____

"It is never too late to be what you might have been."

George Eliot

Date: _____

"Humility is the solid foundation of all virtues."

Confucius

Date: _____

"We have all a better guide in ourselves, if we would attend to it, than any other person can be."

Jane Austen

Date: _____

"Dignity does not consist in possessing honours, but in deserving them."

Aristotle

Date: _____

"Don't worry when you are not recognized but strive to be worthy of recognition."

Abraham Lincoln

Date: _____

"When you arise in the morning, think of what a precious privilege it is to be alive - to breathe, to think, to enjoy, to love."

Marcus Aurelius

Date: _____

"You must be the change you wish to see in the world."

Gandhi

Date: _____

"The most worth-while thing is to try to put happiness into the lives of others."

Robert Baden Powell

Date: _____

"The best thing one can do when it's raining is to let it rain."

Henry Wadsworth Longfellow

Date: _____

"Everyone thinks of changing the world, but no one thinks of changing himself."

Leo Tolstoy

Date: _____

"Memory is the treasury and guardian of all things."

Marcus Tulius Cicero

Date: _____

"Wherever you go, go with all your heart."

Confucius

Date: _____

"Energy and persistence conquer all things."

Benjamin Franklin

Date: _____

"What really matters is what you do with what you have."

H.G. Wells

Date: _____

" I attribute my success to this - I never gave or took any excuse."

Florence Nightingale

Date: _____

"Every great dream begins with a dreamer. Always remember, you have within you the strength, the patience, and the passion to reach for the stars to change the world."

Harriet Tubman

Date: _____

"Nothing strengthens the judgment and quickens the conscience like individual responsibility."

Elizabeth Cady Stanton

Date: _____

"Be thou the rainbow in the storms of life. The evening beam that smiles the clouds away, and tints tomorrow with prophetic ray."

Lord Byron

Date: _____

"One secret of success in life is for a man to be ready for his opportunity when it comes."

Benjamin Disraeli

Date: _____

"The really great man is the man who makes every man feel great."

G. K. Chesterton

Date: _____

"Dreams are illustrations from the book your soul is writing about you."

Marsha Norman

Date:

"Great things are not done by impulse, but by a series of small things brought together."

Vincent van Gogh

Date:

_____

"It isn't what we say that defines us but what we do."

Jane Austen

Date: _____

"Of you don't know where you are going, any road will take you there"

Lewis Caroll

Date:

"Knowing others is wisdom, knowing yourself is Enlightenment"

Lao Tzu

Date:

Reflections on your month of journaling

What went well for you this month and why was this?

_____

_____

_____

What didn't go well for you and why?

_____

_____

_____

What would you have done differently?

_____

_____

_____

How will you adopt this habit in the future?

_____

_____

_____

Now again, on a scale of 1 to 10, where 1 is totally miserable and 10 is blissfully happy, what would you rate your level of happiness right now?

Today my happiness score is: ____

Is there any difference between when you started the month and when you finished the month?

Did journaling increase your sense of happiness?

_____

_____

_____

Why do you think that was?

_____

_____

_____

Month 8 - Visualisation

Minds are like parachutes.

They only function when they are open.

Sir James Dewar

Month 8 is our month to develop the visualisation habit. If this is something new to you, then let me explain what it is and why it's an important habit to get into.

What is visualisation?

Visualisation (also known as mental imagery or visual mental rehearsal) is a technique whereby you mentally picture yourself doing something.

It may sound crazy, but your mind can actually be programmed for success. Research published in North American Journal of Psychology in 2007 compared three groups of athletes: the first group mentally practiced a specific exercise, the next group actually did it, the third group did neither. The first group (who only mentally practiced the task remember) increased their strength by 24%, the second by 28%, the third had no difference. (Reference: Erin M. Shackell and Lionel G. Standing, "Mind Over Matter: Mental Training Increases Physical Strength," North American Journal of Psychology, 2007, Vol. 9, No. 1, 189—200.).

Taking time each day to mentally go through all the actions needed to carry out the exercise, was almost as good as actually doing it. The body didn't realise the difference.

What does this mean for you? Well, visualisation is a tool used by athletes and people looking for success to pre-programme their minds for success. So why not start programming yourself for the life you want?

Hal Elrod in his book The Miracle Morning suggested this technique for visualisation:

1. Prepare yourself, by putting on some quiet meditation music on in the background. Then get comfortable.
2. In your minds eye, picture everything you want. Forget about the practicalities for the moment. If there were no limits, what would the life you want look like. What are you doing, what was the outcome? What did you want to happen?
3. Now visualise the person you must become to make that happen, and what do you need to do to get there. Writers write, singers sing, athletes' practice, and entrepreneurs hustle. What do you need to do?

If you're not sure, research the people that are already doing it. Chris Hatfield, the astronaut, modelled everything he did on those very first astronauts. He became a pilot, then test pilot and so on until he applied to become an astronaut. You can do this too.

There's one thing that I've realised over time, and that is this. Everywhere around the world, there are ordinary people doing what you would call extraordinary things:

- A blind person and several amputees have climbed Mount Everest
- disabled people take part in marathons
- people with learning disabilities who were previously institutionalised now have fulfilling lives.

When you hold yourself back, look around and see what other people are doing.

What makes them different?

1. They have a dream.
2. They believe they can do it.
3. They focus on the prize.
4. They surround themselves with people who help them.
5. They're not afraid to ask for help.
6. They've failed at some point.
7. They got up stronger.

Use your visualisation month to:

- Get clear on what you want.
- Picture it.
- Work out who you have to be to have it.
- Want it badly enough that you make changes to become that person.
- Create an action plan to get you there.
- Start.

Using vision boards

Another thing you could do this month is create a vision board of all the things you want in your life, who you want to be etc.

I've created my vision board on PowerPoint and saved it as the background image on my laptop.

Each one of these images is a goal for me to complete, and as such, I create little action plans and to do lists to make it happen.

Give it a go yourself.

Planning for success

What are the benefits of trying this habit?

_____

_____

What things might stop you this month?

_____

_____

What could you do about them to stop them being a problem?

_____

_____

How will you know you've been successful this month?

_____

_____

How will you reward yourself for that success?

_____

_____

"The reward of a thing well done is to have done it"
Ralph Waldo Emmerson

Week commencing: _____

Monday

Today I visualised

Tuesday

Today I visualised

Wednesday

Today I visualised

Thursday

Today I visualised

Friday

Today I visualised

Saturday

Today I visualised

Sunday

Today I visualised

"The highest reward for a man's toil is not what he gets for it, but what he becomes by it"

John Ruskin

Week commencing: _____

Monday

Today I visualised

Tuesday

Today I visualised

Wednesday

Today I visualised

Thursday

Today I visualised

Friday

Today I visualised

Saturday

Today I visualised

Sunday

Today I visualised

"Turn your face to the sun and the shadows fall behind you"

Maori proverb

Week commencing: _____

Monday
Today I visualised

Tuesday
Today I visualised

Wednesday
Today I visualised

Thursday

Today I visualised

Friday

Today I visualised

Saturday

Today I visualised

Sunday

Today I visualised

"Believe you can, and you're halfway there."
Theodore Roosevelt

Week commencing: _____

Monday
Today I visualised

Tuesday
Today I visualised

Wednesday
Today I visualised

Thursday

Today I visualised

Friday

Today I visualised

Saturday

Today I visualised

Sunday

Today I visualised

"Start by doing what's necessary; then do what's possible; and suddenly you are doing the impossible."

Francis of Assisi

Week commencing: _____

Monday
Today I visualised

Tuesday
Today I visualised

Wednesday
Today I visualised

Thursday

Today I visualised

Friday

Today I visualised

Saturday

Today I visualised

Sunday

Today I visualised

Reflections on your month of visualisation

What went well for you this month and why was this?

_____

_____

_____

What didn't go well for you and why?

_____

_____

_____

What would you have done differently?

_____

_____

_____

How will you adopt this habit in the future?

_____

_____

_____

Now again, on a scale of 1 to 10, where 1 is totally miserable and 10 is blissfully happy, what would you rate your level of happiness right now?

Today my happiness score is: ____

Is there any difference between when you started the month and when you finished the month?

Did practicing visualisation increase your sense of happiness?

_____

_____

_____

Why do you think that was?

_____

_____

_____

Month 9 - Optimism

"Optimist: day dreamer more elegantly spelled.

Mark Twain

Month 9 is your month to develop the optimism habit. Why optimism? Well, optimistic people tend to be happier and healthier, and whilst it may be hard to stay positive all the time, even negative people can be optimistic.

What is optimism?

Optimism is an attitude of hopefulness.

Optimism v Positivity

Optimism tends to go with positivity, however, there is a very subtle difference between the two. A positive person may sometimes be blind to the negative side of things, either not wanting to see them or ignoring them completely, whilst an optimistic person is aware of them, can see the reality of a situation, but still remains hopeful.

Optimists v Pessimists

Martin Seligman identified 3 differences between optimists and pessimists:

- Optimists see problems as temporary, pessimists as permanent.
- Optimists see problems individually, pessimists make them a general case.
- Optimists will look for causes not necessarily themselves, pessimists tend to blame themselves.

In order to move towards a more optimistic mindset, he suggests that you reflect on what happened, trying to see it more objectively. Think about what happened, what your belief around this was and what was the consequence of your belief. Then ask, is this a true reflection of what happened?

To read more about this, check out Learned Optimism by Martin Seligman.

Positive Affirmations v Optimistic Affirmations

When I first started mind-mapping the 12 habits I wanted to develop, this month was the habit of positive affirmations.

However, not everyone is comfortable using positive affirmations.

They may feel a little false to you, but if you do like them, then check out Louse Hay and Hal Elrod, both their websites and their books are very helpful and have many examples of positive affirmations. Choose the affirmations that appeal to you, then repeat them each morning.

Optimistic affirmations are slightly different. Personally, when I say a positive affirmation, my self-limiting beliefs rise-up and my good intentions are jinxed.

Whereas with optimistic affirmations, I recognise that things aren't perfect, but I am hopeful that things will get better. For this reason, optimistic affirmations tend to be more honest and rooted in fact.

A positive affirmation may say:

"I am unlimited in my wealth. All areas of my life are abundant and fulfilling" – Louise Hay

Whereas an optimistic affirmation might say:

"I know my bank account is low, but I can make enough money today to see me through."

It's up to you whether you use positive affirmations or optimistic ones, the point is to start your day on a positive note.

How can you practice optimism this month?

There are several actions that you can take to help you feel more optimistic this month.

Feel free to add to this list:

- Start the day by saying a positive or optimistic affirmation each morning.
- Visualise a positive day, with everything going right, then visualise plan B where some things may go wrong, but you have a backup plan to overcome these obstacles.
- Like positive things on social media and change your settings so that positive things are shown first in your timeline.
- Use your journal to record the positive things that went on your day.
- Keep up your gratitude journal.
- Spend more time with positive people.
- Be mindful of how you talk to others and how you talk about yourself. Don't put yourself down.
- Practice kindness this month and be mindful of the positive effect it has on you.
- Smile. The world might just smile back.

Planning for success

What are the benefits of trying this habit?

_____

_____

What things might stop you this month?

_____

_____

What could you do about them to stop them being a problem?

_____

_____

How will you know you've been successful this month?

_____

_____

How will you reward yourself for that success?

_____

_____

"Our greatest glory is not in never falling, but in rising every time we fall."

Confucius

Week commencing: _____

Monday

> Today I was optimistic

Tuesday

> Today I was optimistic

Wednesday

> Today I was optimistic

Thursday

Today I was optimistic

Friday

Today I was optimistic

Saturday

Today I was optimistic

Sunday

Today I was optimistic

"Pessimism leads to weakness, optimism to power."
William James

Week commencing: _____

Monday
> Today I was optimistic

Tuesday
> Today I was optimistic

Wednesday
> Today I was optimistic

Thursday

Today I was optimistic

Friday

Today I was optimistic

Saturday

Today I was optimistic

Sunday

Today I was optimistic

"Optimism is essential to achievement and it is also the foundation of courage and true progress."

Nicholas M Butler

Week commencing: _____

Monday

Today I was optimistic

Tuesday

Today I was optimistic

Wednesday

Today I was optimistic

Thursday

Today I was optimistic

Friday

Today I was optimistic

Saturday

Today I was optimistic

Sunday

Today I was optimistic

"There are two ways of spreading light: to be the candle or the mirror that reflects it."

Edith Wharton

Week commencing: _____

Monday
Today I was optimistic

Tuesday
Today I was optimistic

Wednesday
Today I was optimistic

Thursday

Today I was optimistic

Friday

Today I was optimistic

Saturday

Today I was optimistic

Sunday

Today I was optimistic

"What lies behind you and what lies in front of you, pales in comparison to what lies inside of you."
Ralph Waldo Emerson

Week commencing: _____

Monday
Today I was optimistic

Tuesday
Today I was optimistic

Wednesday
Today I was optimistic

Thursday

Today I was optimistic

Friday

Today I was optimistic

Saturday

Today I was optimistic

Sunday

Today I was optimistic

Reflections on your month of optimism

What went well for you this month and why was this?

_____

_____

_____

What didn't go well for you and why?

_____

_____

_____

What would you have done differently?

_____

_____

_____

How will you adopt this habit in the future?

_____

_____

_____

Now again, on a scale of 1 to 10, where 1 is totally miserable and 10 is blissfully happy, what would you rate your level of happiness right now?

Today my happiness score is: ____

Is there any difference between when you started the month and when you finished the month?

Did practicing optimism increase your sense of happiness?

_____

_____

_____

Why do you think that was?

_____

_____

_____

Month 10 - Learning

Tell me and I forget.

Teach me and I remember.

Involve me and I learn.

Benjamin Franklin

Month 10 is your month to develop the learning habit.

Why develop the learning habit?

The most successful people on the planet make time to read every day, learning and developing all the time.

This may be for 15 minutes in the morning or a few hours each day. Instead of watching tv, they learn. Reading allows them to learn about new ideas, the lives of other people and about themselves.

However, as a home-schooling mum of a dyslexic child, I recognise that learning is not just about reading books.

These days we have so many more options to feed the mind. Books are available as audiobooks, plays and movies. You can attend conferences and listen to speakers. You can watch or download documentaries or learn a new skill via YouTube.

As part of our home school, we use a massive range of learning resources:

- Books
- Audiobooks
- Podcasts
- Blogs
- TED talks
- YouTube
- Tv documentaries
- Online courses
- Experiment kits
- Music and sports classes
- Field trips

- Visits to museums, zoos and heritage sites

The list is endless. If there's something you've always wanted to do or learn more about, now's your chance.

How will the learning habit make me happy?

There is a certain joy in stepping outside your comfort zone and doing something that you thought you couldn't.

Anything is possible, but our own self-limiting beliefs very often stop us before we even start.

The problem with schools is they very often take away any joy in learning, but as human being we have an innate sense of curiosity.

By tapping into it, and trying something new, especially if it is something that scares us, we move outside our comfort zone and widen it.

So, this month, try to do or learn something that you haven't tried before. If you have a natural affinity for one of the intelligences, then try another.

Howard Gardner in his 1983 book, Frames of Mind: The Theory of Multiple Intelligences identified nine intelligences: nature, music, logic/maths, existential, interpersonal, body movement e.g. gymnastics, athletics, dance, intra-personal, special and languages.

An example might be someone who is drawn to nature trying to learn dancing or a language.

Think about what you could try, just for a month.

Getting started

To get started, think about what it is you'd like to learn about. Once you're clear on this, you can start planning HOW you're going to learn about it, what resources you need and how you can access them.

You may want to learn a new skill, a new language, download a new podcast, follow a new blog or simply want to read some self-help books. Either way, the choice is yours. Just set aside at least 15 minutes each day to focus on your personal development.

This month, I'd like to learn more about:

_____

_____

_____

What resources will you need to try this?

_____

_____

_____

Planning for success

What are the benefits of trying this habit?

_____

_____

What things might stop you this month?

_____

_____

What could you do about them to stop them being a problem?

_____

_____

How will you know you've been successful this month?

_____

_____

How will you reward yourself for that success?

_____

_____

"Live as if you were to die tomorrow. Learn as if you were to live forever."

Mahatma Gandhi

Week commencing: _____

Monday

Today, I learnt

Tuesday

Today, I learnt

Wednesday

Today, I learnt

Thursday

Today, I learnt

Friday

Today, I learnt

Saturday

Today, I learnt

Sunday

Today, I learnt

"You cannot open a book without learning something."

Confucius

Week commencing: _____

Monday

Today, I learnt

Tuesday

Today, I learnt

Wednesday

Today, I learnt

Thursday

Today, I learnt

Friday

Today, I learnt

Saturday

Today, I learnt

Sunday

Today, I learnt

"Learning is not attained by chance. It must be sought for with ardor and attended to with diligence."

Abigail Adams

Week commencing: _____

Monday
Today, I learnt

Tuesday
Today, I learnt

Wednesday
Today, I learnt

Thursday

Today, I learnt

Friday

Today, I learnt

Saturday

Today, I learnt

Sunday

Today, I learnt

"Never let formal education get in the way of your learning."

Mark Twain

Week commencing: _____

Monday
Today, I learnt

Tuesday
Today, I learnt

Wednesday
Today, I learnt

Thursday

Today, I learnt

Friday

Today, I learnt

Saturday

Today, I learnt

Sunday

Today, I learnt

"The love of learning, the sequestered nooks, And all the sweet serenity of books."

Henry Wadsworth Longfellow

Week commencing: _____

Monday

Today, I learnt

Tuesday

Today, I learnt

Wednesday

Today, I learnt

Thursday

Today, I learnt

Friday

Today, I learnt

Saturday

Today, I learnt

Sunday

Today, I learnt

Reflections on your month of learning

What went well for you this month and why was this?

_____

_____

_____

What didn't go well for you and why?

_____

_____

_____

What would you have done differently?

_____

_____

_____

How will you adopt this habit in the future?

_____

_____

_____

Now again, on a scale of 1 to 10, where 1 is totally miserable and 10 is blissfully happy, what would you rate your level of happiness right now?

Today my happiness score is: ____

Is there any difference between when you started the month and when you finished the month?

Did learning new things increase your sense of happiness?

_____

_____

_____

Why do you think that was?

_____

_____

_____

Month 11 - Creativity

Happiness lies in the joy of achievement and the thrill of creative effort.

Franklin D. Roosevelt

Month 11 is your month to focus on developing your creativity.

Why be creative?

As kids, we got to be creative all the time. It was actually expected of us.

We were given crafts, toys and games that enabled us to make stuff and fuel our imagination.

However, as we got older, our inner critic (and sometimes criticism from others) took over, and somewhere along the way we stopped. We may have lost our confidence, or we may have become so busy that opportunities to be creative became less and less.

Whatever the reason, for many of us, we are less creative now than we've ever been.

How does being creative make you happy?

As human beings, we are creative creatures by nature. You only have to think about the cave drawings from 40,000 years ago to realise that this is true.

Creativity allows us to express ourselves, relax and in addition, research suggests that creativity and innovation may even part of our survival mechanisms as a species.

Whatever the reasons, there is a certain joy is making something new, from scratch.

Making time to be creative makes us happy.

What does "being creative" mean to you?

Before you start on your month of creativity, it's important to be clear on what we mean by being creative. When I looked it up, words and phrases like these came up:

- Making something new
- Using your imagination
- Solving a problem
- Making up stories
- Inventing something
- Having new ideas.

Whichever way you define creative or creativity, it's time to stretch yourself. Whether it's:

- trying some arts and crafts
- making up a bedtime story for your kids
- writing a poem or short story
- making a video
- cooking something from scratch
- or something else entirely.

You have a whole month to try, so use your imagination and perhaps have some fun at the same time.

Before you start, here are some journal prompts to help you rediscover your inner creative spirit.

For me, being creative means...

_____

_____

_____

_____

_____

_____

In the past, I was creative when I...

_____

_____

_____

_____

_____

_____

_____

Planning for success

What are the benefits of trying this habit?

_____

_____

What things might stop you this month?

_____

_____

What could you do about them to stop them being a problem?

_____

_____

How will you know you've been successful this month?

_____

_____

How will you reward yourself for that success?

_____

_____

"Odd how the creative power at once brings the whole universe to order."

Virginia Woolf

Week commencing: _____

Monday

Today I was creative by

Tuesday

Today I was creative by

Wednesday

Today I was creative by

Thursday

Today I was creative by

Friday

Today I was creative by

Saturday

Today I was creative by

Sunday

Today I was creative by

"True happiness comes from the joy of deeds well done, the zest of creating things new."

Antoine de Saint-Exupery

Week commencing: _____

Monday

Today I was creative by

Tuesday

Today I was creative by

Wednesday

Today I was creative by

Thursday

Today I was creative by

Friday

Today I was creative by

Saturday

Today I was creative by

Sunday

Today I was creative by

"Great indeed is the sublimity of the Creative, to which all beings owe their beginning, and which permeates all heaven. "

Lao Tzu

Week commencing: _____

Monday

Today I was creative by

Tuesday

Today I was creative by

Wednesday

Today I was creative by

Thursday

Today I was creative by

Friday

Today I was creative by

Saturday

Today I was creative by

Sunday

Today I was creative by

"I dream my painting and paint my dream."
Vincent van Gogh

Week commencing: _____

Monday

Today I was creative by

Tuesday

Today I was creative by

Wednesday

Today I was creative by

Thursday

Today I was creative by

Friday

Today I was creative by

Saturday

Today I was creative by

Sunday

Today I was creative by

"Music gives a soul to the universe, wings to the mind, flight to the imagination and life to everything."

Plato

Week commencing: _____

Monday

Today I was creative by

Tuesday

Today I was creative by

Wednesday

Today I was creative by

Thursday

Today I was creative by

Friday

Today I was creative by

Saturday

Today I was creative by

Sunday

Today I was creative by

Reflections on your month of creativity

What went well for you this month and why was this?

_____

_____

_____

What didn't go well for you and why?

_____

_____

_____

What would you have done differently?

_____

_____

_____

How will you adopt this habit in the future?

_____

_____

_____

Now again, on a scale of 1 to 10, where 1 is totally miserable and 10 is blissfully happy, what would you rate your level of happiness right now?

Today my happiness score is: ____

Is there any difference between when you started the month and when you finished the month?

Did being creative increase your sense of happiness?

_____

_____

_____

Why do you think that was?

_____

_____

_____

Month 12 - Fun

Keep love in your heart.

A life without it is like a sunless garden when the flowers are dead.

Oscar Wilde

Month 12 is our month to remember how to have fun.

This habit is one that is very close to my heart.

On the first day of my life coaching course, we were asked to use the wheel of life and rate each section on a scale of 1 to 10. When it came to fun, I was totally lost. I couldn't even say what fun was. How on earth had I gotten to that place?

I realised that somewhere along the way, I'd gotten on a hamster wheel of work, housework, homework, caring and sleep. I didn't have time for fun even when I needed it.

As part of the coaching process, I had to sit back and really think about what fun was for me, and how I could incorporate in my life.

Now I make sure that I inject fun into most things I do in my life.

Why having fun is important for your happiness?

Quite simply because it provides balance in our busy lives. We need fun to offset all the stresses that come into our lives.

Without fun, our lives are busy but empty.

How do you define fun?

I don't mean the dictionary definition, I mean what are you doing when you have fun. It's different for all of us, so take a minute to be clear on what it is for you.

Fun for me is...

_____

_____

_____

_____

I'm having fun when I...

When was the last time you truly had fun, what were you doing, who were you with and where?

NB: If you struggle with this, check in with the group.

_____

_____

_____

_____

_____

_____

_____

_____

_____

_____

_____

_____

Now take a look at what you've written. What does it tell you about yourself?

Next, on a scale of 1 to 10, (where 1 is "what's fun?" and 10 is "having the most fun ever") how much fun do you have in your life at this moment in time:

At this very moment, my fun level is:

Then at the end of the month, review this score and see if it has increased?

At the end of this month, my fun level is:

Planning for success

What are the benefits of trying this habit?

_____

_____

What things might stop you this month?

_____

_____

What could you do about them to stop them being a problem?

_____

_____

How will you know you've been successful this month?

_____

_____

How will you reward yourself for that success?

_____

_____

"The price of anything is the amount of life you exchange for it."

Henry David Thoreau

Week commencing: _____

Monday
Today, I had fun because

Tuesday
Today was a fun day

Wednesday
Today, I had fun with

Thursday

Today, I had fun at

Friday

Today, I had fun because

Saturday

Today, I had fun with

Sunday

Today was a fun day

"Time spent laughing is time spent with the Gods."
Japanese proverb

Week commencing: _____

Monday
Today, I had fun because

Tuesday
Today was a fun day

Wednesday
Today, I had fun with

Thursday

Today, I had fun at

Friday

Today, I had fun because

Saturday

Today, I had fun with

Sunday

Today was a fun day

"Life is too important to take seriously."

Oscar Wilde

Week commencing: _____

Monday

Today, I had fun because

Tuesday

Today was a fun day

Wednesday

Today, I had fun with

Thursday

Today, I had fun at

Friday

Today, I had fun because

Saturday

Today, I had fun with

Sunday

Today was a fun day

"Always laugh when you can. It's cheap medicine."
Lord Byron

Week commencing: _____

Monday

Today, I had fun because

Tuesday

Today was a fun day

Wednesday

Today, I had fun with

Thursday

Today, I had fun at

Friday

Today, I had fun because

Saturday

Today, I had fun with

Sunday

Today was a fun day

"A good laugh is sunshine in the house."
William Makepeace Thackeray

Week commencing: _____

Monday

> Today, I had fun because

Tuesday

> Today was a fun day

Wednesday

> Today, I had fun with

Thursday

Today, I had fun at

Friday

Today, I had fun because

Saturday

Today, I had fun with

Sunday

Today was a fun day

Reflections on your month of fun

What went well for you this month and why was this?

_____

_____

_____

What didn't go well for you and why?

_____

_____

_____

What would you have done differently?

_____

_____

_____

How will you adopt this habit in the future?

_____

_____

_____

Now again, on a scale of 1 to 10, where 1 is totally miserable and 10 is blissfully happy, what would you rate your level of happiness right now?

Today my happiness score is: ___

Is there any difference between when you started the month and when you finished the month?

Did making fun a priority increase your sense of happiness?

_____

_____

_____

Why do you think that was?

_____

_____

_____

What I've learnt from my Happy Habits year...

Congratulations.

If you have completed this journal, you'll be well on the way to building positive habits that will enable your future happiness.

Tomorrow is the beginning of a whole new year, with new opportunities just waiting for you.

If you've enjoyed this journal, then you may want to try building more positive habits. Check me out on Amazon and see what other journals I've developed:

www.amazon.co.uk/Karen-Brown/e/B00AXAF2M8

And if you've enjoyed this book, then I'd love to hear what helped most. I'd also be really grateful if you'd leave a review on Amazon.

Take care for now. And thank you for sharing this journey with me.

Karen x

35478113R00141

Printed in Poland
by Amazon Fulfillment
Poland Sp. z o.o., Wrocław